TUNNELING EARTHWORMS

by Suzanne Paul Dell'Oro

Lerner Publications Company • Minneapolis

This book is available in two editions:
Library binding by Lerner Publications Company, a division of Lerner Publishing Group
Soft cover by First Avenue Editions, an imprint of Lerner Publishing Group
241 First Avenue North
Minneapolis, MN 55401 U.S.A.

Website address: www.lernerbooks.com

Words in *italic type* are explained in a glossary
on page 30.

Library of Congress Cataloging-in-Publication Data

Dell'Oro, Suzanne Paul.
    Tunneling earthworms / by Suzanne Paul Dell'Oro.
      p. cm. — (Pull ahead books)
    Includes index.
    Summary: Describes the habitat, physical
characteristics, and behavior of earthworms.
    ISBN 0-8225-3762-1 (lib. bdg. : alk. paper)—
    ISBN 0-8225-3768-0 (pbk. : alk. paper)
    1. Earthworms—Juvenile literature. [1. Earthworms.]
    I. Title. II. Series.
QL391.A6 D44 2001
592'.64—dc–21   00-008006

Manufactured in the United States of America
1 2 3 4 5 6 — JR — 06 05 04 03 02 01

What animal is tunneling
into the ground?

This is an earthworm.
An earthworm has a long, thin body.

Most earthworms live in
underground tunnels called *burrows.*

What is it like underground?

It is dark, cool, and wet underground.

Earthworms stay there because they must keep their skin from drying out.

An earthworm's skin is coated with slime called *mucus.*

The wet mucus lets earthworms breathe and drink through their skin.

Sunlight dries out an earthworm's skin.

So earthworms come out of the ground only at night and on rainy days.

During cold winters, earthworms rest together deep in their burrows.

During hot summers, they tunnel down to find soil that is wet.

Tunneling is easy for an earthworm!
Its body is just right.

The slippery mucus on its body helps
an earthworm move through the soil.

Segments are rings along an earthworm's body.

Segments help an earthworm stretch and change shape.

An earthworm stretches out
when it moves.

It grabs the dirt with its front end,
then its back end slides forward.

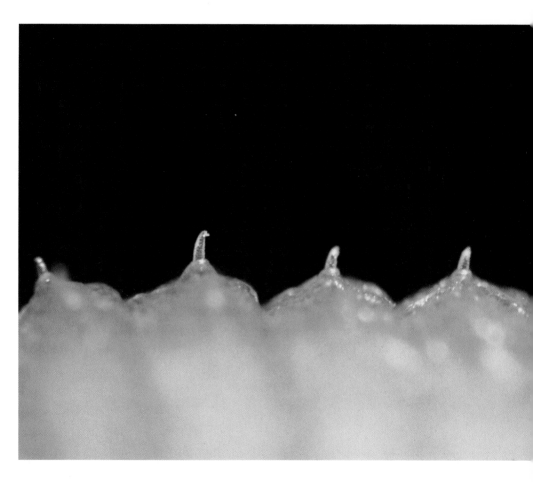

Tiny *bristles* on its skin help an earthworm grip the soil.

Earthworms are *invertebrates.*
Invertebrates have no backbones.

An earthworm's soft body lets it
squeeze through cracks in the soil.

Earthworms push their way
underground through the soil.

How do earthworms move
through hard soil?

If the soil is too hard to push aside, earthworms eat their way through!

When they eat the soil, earthworms eat the tiny animals that live in it.

What
else do
earthworms
eat?

Earthworms eat dead plants, animals, and bugs!

They swallow soil with their food.

The soil leaves the earthworm's body in small piles called *castings.*

You may find castings on the ground around an earthworm's burrow.

Sometimes an earthworm pulls food into its burrow, like this leaf.

The leaf keeps out hot air and hides the burrow from enemies.

Many animals try to eat earthworms.
The earthworm clings to the ground.

An earthworm's enemies have a
hard time pulling it out of the soil.

If an enemy bites off the tail of an earthworm, the tail may grow back.

Some earthworms can even grow a new head!

An earthworm's head has no eyes, ears, or nose.

Which end of this earthworm is its head?

The head is more pointed than the tail.
Around the middle of the earthworm,

there is a bulge called the *clitellum*.
The clitellum is closer to the head.

An earthworm's clitellum
makes *cocoons.*

Cocoons are small packages that
are full of eggs.

An adult earthworm leaves cocoons in the ground.

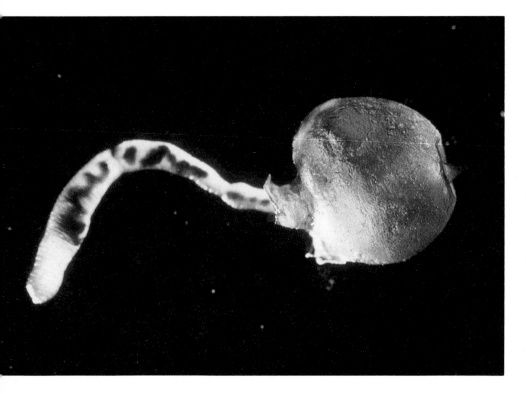

A baby earthworm comes out of each egg in the cocoon.

The babies look just like adults,
but they are very tiny.

They tunnel and eat right away to
start their life underground.

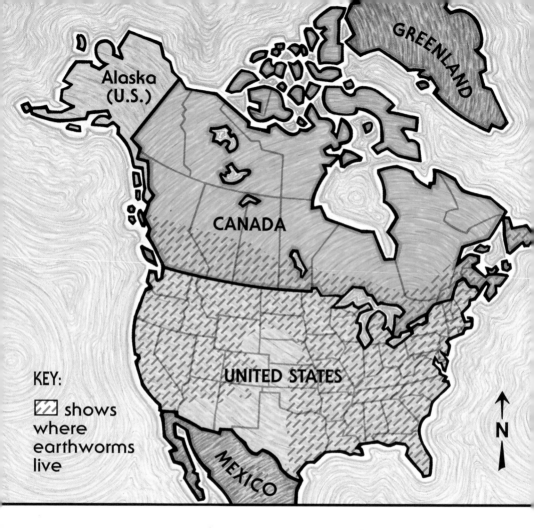

KEY:

 shows where earthworms live

Find your state or province on this map.
Do earthworms live near you?

Parts of an Earthworm's Body

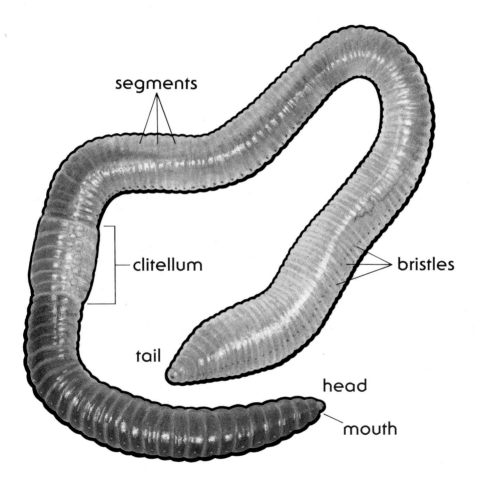

segments

clitellum

bristles

tail

head

mouth

Glossary

bristles: tiny, strong hairs that help an earthworm grip the soil

burrows: underground tunnels where earthworms live

castings: piles of soil that leave an earthworm's body after the earthworm eats

clitellum: the bulge on an earthworm's body that makes cocoons

cocoons: packages that an animal makes that have an egg or eggs inside

invertebrates: animals that have no backbones

mucus: slime that covers an earthworm's skin and helps keep it wet

segments: rings around an earthworm's body that help it move

Hunt and Find

- a **baby earthworm** on pages 26–27
- an earthworm **burrow** on pages 5, 15, 16, 20
- earthworm **cocoons** on pages 25, 26
- an earthworm **eating** on pages 16–18, 20
- an **enemy** of earthworms on page 21
- an earthworm **growing a new tail** on page 22
- earthworms **resting** together on page 9

The publisher wishes to thank to our **series consultant,** Sharyn Fenwick. An elementary science-math specialist, Mrs. Fenwick was the recipient of the National Science Teachers Association 1991 Distinguished Teaching Award. In 1992, representing the state of Minnesota at the elementary level, she received the Presidential Award for Excellence in Math and Science Teaching.

About the Author

Suzanne Paul Dell'Oro lives in St. Paul, Minnesota, with her husband, three children, and the family cat. She loves to work in the garden, where she gets lots of help from earthworms.

Photo Acknowledgments

The photographs in this book are reproduced through the courtesy of: © Robert Clay/Visuals Unlimited, front cover; © Dwight R. Kuhn, back cover, pp. 4, 7, 8, 15, 17, 18, 25, 26, 27, 31; © Stephen P. Parker/The National Audubon Society Collection/Photo Researchers, Inc., p. 3; © J.P. Ferrero /Jacana/The National Audubon Society Collection/Photo Researchers, Inc., p. 5; © William Grenfall/Visuals Unlimited, p. 6; © R. Konig/Jacana/The National Audubon Society Collection/Photo Researchers, Inc., p. 9; © L.West/Bruce Coleman, Inc., p. 10; © Bill Beatty/Visuals Unlimited, p. 11; © Leonard Lee Rue, III/The National Audubon Society Collection/Photo Researchers, Inc., p.12 (both); © Pat Lynch/The National Audubon Society Collection/Photo Researchers, Inc., p. 14; © John Kaprielian/The National Audubon Society Collection/Photo Researchers, Inc., p. 16; © Frank T. Awbrey/Visuals Unlimited, p. 19; © Kathie Atkinson/AUSCAPE, pp. 20, 24; © Alan and Sandy Carey/The National Audubon Society Collection/Photo Researchers, Inc., p. 21; © Cooke, J. A. L. OSF/Animals Animals, p. 22; © E. R. Degginger/ Bruce Coleman, Inc., p. 23.